RECEIVING AND MAINTAINING GOD'S REVIVAL IN YOUR LIFE AND IN THE LOCAL CHURCH.

Volume 1

(Special Bible Study Edition with Study Questions)

(Understanding God's Revivals and Personal Revivals)

STEPHEN ADU-BOAHEN

Table of Contents

INTRODUCTION

Dealing with a subject as important and complex as revivals demands a clear understanding of the major issues at stake right from the beginning to be able to make headway. It is this understanding which will give direction to you on the right path to take and also show you all the important essentials to put together to be able to produce a comprehensible, impactful and fully relevant spiritual document.

In consequence of this, understanding God's revivals which is the first of the series of four books making up this series on God's revivals is very important as the foundational book of these volumes as well as the directional guide on this journey into God's revivals. In the light of this, it mainly deals with rudimentary topics relating to our clear understanding of God's revivals as they touch on definitions of corporate and personal revivals and biblical pictures which give us a clear understanding of what God's revivals entail. Starting with this clear understanding of this great subject is the way to go to be able to finish this journey of gaining deep insight into God-given revivals.

May the good Lord help us on this divine journey towards spiritual renewal after getting a clear understanding of all the intricacies of this great subject in this foundational volume. Read on for a great adventure into God-given revivals!

PART 1

UNDERSTANDING GOD'S REVIVAL IN THE GENERAL SENSE

PREAMBLE

The keywords in every revival programme are "RENEWAL, restitution, Rekindling and Revitalization". The key theological concepts in every genuine quest for God's revival are "SPIRITUAL RENEWAL and Spiritual Revitialization" which break backsliding, compromise with sin and spiritual declension and thereafter lead to an immediate and decisive return to God's ways, values and standards. Whenever and wherever this happens it always results in spiritual elevation, spiritual empowerment, spiritual victory and spiritual success in all areas of the Christian Life. This in short ensures our return to holiness, holy living and to the victorious and successful Christian Life which alone can help us to finish the Christian race successfully and finally conduct us into the holy presence of God in heaven

It is the attainment of these ideals which calls for regular revivals in every vibrant church of the Lord Jesus Christ. The definition, explanation and illustration of this corporate revival is what part one of this book mainly deals with because we need to fully understand what God's genuine revival is before we can seek it with the seriousness and determination it requires. So let us go through this first two chapters with an enquiring mind to be able to grasp all the basic concepts of God's revivals as outlined in this two chapters as follows:

CHAPTER ONE

THE DEFINITION OF REVIVAL

WHAT IS REVIVAL?

This is a big question which must be answered right at the beginning of this book to help its readers to know and be sure of what they are seeking and to be specific in what they are praying for and are trying to promote in their churches. We are going to answer this question in two ways. First, since the word "revival" is an English word, we want to understand it in the English language. Thereafter, we will also try to find a theological definition and explanation for the word "Revival."

SOME DICTIONARY DEFINITIONS OF REVIVAL

A period of renewed religious interest. (Merriam-Webster's Dictionary)

A _time_ when _interest_ in _religion_ _starts_ again in a _stronger_ way than before, or a _meeting_ or _series_ of

<u>meetings</u> <u>organized</u> to <u>encourage</u> this to <u>happen.</u>
(Cambridge Dictionary)

The two English dictionaries quoted above set the tone for our discussion of the meaning and theological significance of revival. While Merriam-Webster generally defines it as a period of renewed religious interest, the Cambridge dictionary goes further to give additional details of what Merriam-Webster calls renewed religious interest. It states this in the words, "…when interest in religion starts in a stronger way than before…" This means that whenever and wherever true revival occurs we move up and forward spiritually and in the things of God. The interesting thing about the two dictionaries is that they both emphasize revival as a period of reawakening and renewal. So Merriam Webster describes it as *"renewed religious interest"* and Cambridge dictionary also describes it as *"a time when interest in religion starts again."* With these two ideas in mind, let us next move on to the theological definitions to see how the Holy Scriptures can amplify these for us to give us some clearly defined levels of practical application.

Bible Study and Personal Review Questions

1. Why is it important for us to try to understand the word "Revival" in the English language at the very beginning of this book?
2. What are some of the dictionary definitions of the word, "Revival?"
3. What do these dictionary definitions emphasize about revival to help us understand it very well?

SOME THEOLOGICAL DEFINITIONS AND EXPLANATIONS OF REVIVAL

The word revival comes from two Latin words, "*vivo*," meaning to live, and "*re*" meaning again. So literally revival means "to live again." This presupposes a time when we were active and full of life in the past. Whatever happened to cause our spiritual death may not be visible to the naked eyes. But with the emergence of revival, the word "re" which means again came to add to the word "vivo" which means to live to cause us to live our former vibrant spiritual lives again! In this, revival becomes similar to words like rebirth and re-awakening. So in summary, true revival signifies a time of spiritual reawakening to shun sin, worldliness, and all other evil attractions to allow the Holy Spirit to move freely in and among believers to set their hearts on fire for the Lord as we learn from Romans 12:11 in the words: "Never lagging behind in diligence; aglow in the Spirit, *enthusiastically* serving the Lord." Amplified Bible.

Explained in different terms, we can also say that revival is a return to our former life of spiritual devotion. It can also be viewed as a reawakening of spiritual fervour which leads to the revitalization of great enthusiasm and passion for the Lord Jesus Christ and the Holy Spirit. Such enthusiasm always leads to the avoidance of sin, great love for holiness and positive Christian virtues as well as a great desire to share the gospel with the lost with the aim of winning them to receive the free salvation God offers. This literally fulfills the great statement of Charles Spurgeon which can be quoted as follows: *"Revival is to live again, to receive again a life which has almost expired, to rekindle into a flame the vital spark which was nearly extinguished."* Matthew 24:12, 13 draws our attention to this truth in the words: *"Because of the increase of wickedness, the love of most will grow cold, but the one who stands firm to the end will be saved."* NIV

After putting all the definitions above together, what summary definition can we give of the word "revival?" The summary includes the following itemized details:

1. *Revival refers to a time of spiritual reawakening. This reawakening always works to bring us out of the state of spiritual dormancy leading to various forms of practical stagnation, inaction and inactivity in our lives as believers.*
2. *True revival always comes with the resurfacing of genuine love for God, a new appreciation of God's absolute holiness, a renewed passion for his Word and His Church and a renewed hatred for sin, evil and all forms of waywardness.*
3. *One great characteristic of true revival is that it always begins with genuine repentance leading to a forsaking of all past sins and acts of rebellion.*
4. *This repentance inevitably leads to a fresh start with God and the Holy Spirit which marks the beginning of a new life lived in total obedience and devotion to God and His values.*

5. *Revival always leads sincere believers to live in the world as they wait for Christ but never to live like the world in worldliness and the pursuit of only carnal desires. This leads us to be able to say with Paul in all sincerity that, "For to me, to live is Christ, and to die is gain" NKJV (Philippians 1:21) which together with the following references elucidate what happens and what to expect whenever any genuine revival from God occurs:*

Psalm 51:10

Create in me a pure heart, O God, and renew a steadfast spirit within me. NKJV

Romans 12:2

Do not conform to the pattern of this world, but be transformed by the renewing of your mind. Then you will be able to test and approve what God's will is — his good, pleasing and perfect will. NIV

Ephesians 4:22-24

You were taught, with regard to your former way of life, to put off your old self, which is being corrupted by its deceitful desires; to be made new in the attitude of your minds; and to put on the new self, created to be like God in true righteousness and holiness. NIV

Bible Study and Personal Review Questions

1. What is the root word of the word "revival" in Latin?

2. When this root word is combined with the English dictionary definitions of revival, what theological definitions can we give of the word "revival" today?

3. From the explanations and definitions given of revival, what specifically should we expect when we say that we are going to seek God's revival?

4. What are the five major truths involved in our truly and genuinely seeking God's revival?

5. Can any of these truths be glossed over if we truly want to receive God's revival? What are the reasons for your answer?

6. What light do the references at the end of this section throw on what we should expect when we say that we are seeking God's revival?

REVIVALS AND THE CONCEPTS OF RENEWAL, NEWNESS AND NEW BEGINNINGS

In seeking to define and understand revivals generally, it is important to note that all the revivals granted by the Godhead – Father, Son and the Holy Spirit can occur only in three major areas. First, they can occur at the personal level in the lives of the individual members of the church. Secondly, they can occur at the general church level when it spreads from the individually revived members of the church into the church as a whole. Thirdly, they can spread from these individual members of the church and from the church itself into the communities in which these revived churches are situated. One dominant proof which emerges any time and anywhere these revivals occur is the concept of spiritual renewal, spiritual revitalization and spiritual freshness from the state of spiritual coldness.

The only difference is that the results and reactions to the revivals differ depending upon where the spiritual reinvigoration takes place. In sinful and unconverted communities, this leads naturally to repentance, a search for the salvation of God and the new life which always accompanies salvation. At the general church level, this can bring renewed commitment to Christ, rededication, a return to personal holiness and sanctification and a new zeal for evangelism. At the individual level, this can lead to a renewed interest in the spiritual things of God like prayerfulness, avoidance of worldly values and worldly amusements, devoting more time to devotional Bible study and the acquisition of a new zeal for God and His work as well as a return to heavenly-mindedness which inevitably leads to separation from all forms of evil and evil associations.

It is therefore important to emphasize in the light of the forgone that the definition and explanation of spiritual revivals in this first chapter of this book is applicable both to personal revivals obtained at the personal and individual levels and to corporate revivals obtained at the general church level. The ideas of spiritual renewal, spiritual newness and a new beginning brought by all genuine revivals are inherent in both of them.

As a supplement to this definition of revival and as an attempt to help us to get a deeper understanding of what revival is all about, we want to quote other definitions of revival directly from several other authentic Christian sources before we end this chapter. The details of what we are saying can be presented as follows:

Bible Study and Personal Review Questions

1. When we talk about revivals, in which three major areas should we expect them to occur?
2. What are the major concepts of revivals which should always be born in mind anytime we are praying for them?
3. Anytime we pray for revivals to occur in the three major areas where they normally break out, what practical results should we expect from these three areas?
4. Anytime we pray for God's revivals to come down at the individual, corporate, and community levels, what is the one key and common feature we must expect in all these three areas and why?

DEFINITIONS OF "REVIVAL" FROM SOME AUTHENTIC CHRISTIAN SOURCES

As already indicated in the preface, revival is an important subject in the life of the New Testament Church. So it must be fully understood and eagerly pursued in the everyday ministry of the Church from the local church to all the important levels of church hierarchy and administration. In the attempt to bring out this full understanding in this book on revival, several authentic and acceptable Christian sources will be quoted. The various sources accessed, gleaned and assessed from reliable contemporary Christian literature are quoted and put together as follows:

Revive is the translation of chayah, "to live," "cause to live," used of restoration to life (Genesis 45:27; Judges 15:19, etc.); of rebuilding (Nehemiah 4:2); of restoration to well-being (Psalms 85:6 (the Revised Version (British and American) "quicken"); Psalms 138:7; Isaiah 57:15; Hosea 6:2); of Yahweh's gracious work for His people (Habakkuk 3:2, "revive thy work in the midst of the years," etc.); "reviving" is the translation of michydh "preservation" or "means of life" (Ezra 9:8,9). "Revive" occurs in the New Testament as the translation of anazao, "to live again" (Romans 7:9; 14:9)... In 1 Macc 13:7 the Revised Version (British and American) we have "And the spirit of the people revived," anazopureo, "to stir or kindle up as a fire," the same word as in 2 Timothy 1:6, the Revised Version

(British and American) "stir up the gift of God, which is in thee," margin "Greek: 'stir into flame.'"

In view of the frequent modern use of "revive" and "revival," it is worthy of notice that it is to Timothy himself the exhortation is addressed. We too often merely pray for "revivals," forgetting that it is for us to "stir into flame" the gift of the Spirit which we have already received of God. It is ours from Him, but we let it lie dormant, as a slumbering ember merely.

W. L. Walker

Copyright Statement

These files are public domain.

Bibliography Information

Orr, James, M.A., D.D. General Editor. "Entry for 'REVIVE; REVIVING'". "International Standard Bible Encyclopedia". 1915.

Quoted Bible References

Genesis 45:27
But when they told him everything Joseph had said to them, and when he saw the carts Joseph had sent to carry him back, the spirit of their father Jacob revived. NIV

Judges 15:19

Then God opened up the hollow place in Lehi, and water came out of it. When Samson drank, his strength returned and he revived. So the spring was called En Hakkore, and it is still there in Lehi. NIV

Nehemiah 4:2

And in the presence of his associates and the army of Samaria, he said, "What are those feeble Jews doing? Will they restore their wall? Will they offer sacrifices? Will they finish in a day? Can they bring the stones back to life from those heaps of rubble — burned as they are?" NIV

Psalms 85:6

Will you not revive us again, that your people may rejoice in you? NIV

Psalms 138:7

Though I walk in the midst of trouble, you preserve my life. You stretch out your hand against the anger of my foes; with your right hand you save me. NIV

Isaiah 57:15

For this is what the high and exalted One says — he who lives forever, whose name is holy: "I live in a high and holy place, but also with the one who is contrite and

lowly in spirit, to revive the spirit of the lowly and to revive the heart of the contrite. NIV

Hosea 6:2
After two days he will revive us; on the third day he will restore us, that we may live in his presence. NIV

Habakkuk 3:2
Lord, I have heard of your fame; I stand in awe of your deeds, Lord. Repeat them in our day, in our time make them known; in wrath remember mercy. NIV

Ezra 9:8, 9
"But now, for a brief moment, the Lord our God has been gracious in leaving us a remnant and giving us a firm place in his sanctuary, and so our God gives light to our eyes and a little relief in our bondage. Though we are slaves, our God has not forsaken us in our bondage. He has shown us kindness in the sight of the kings of Persia: He has granted us new life to rebuild the house of our God and repair its ruins, and he has given us a wall of protection in Judah and Jerusalem. NIV

Romans 7:9
Once I was alive apart from the law; but when the commandment came, sin sprang to life and I died. NIV

Romans 14:9

For this very reason, Christ died and returned to life so that he might be the Lord of both the dead and the living.
NIV

VARIOUS OTHER DEFINITIONS OF REVIVAL/SPIRITUAL AWAKENING

"God's quickening visitation of his people, touching their hearts and deepening his work of grace in their lives." J. I. Packer

"The sovereign act of God, in which He restores His own backsliding people to repentance, faith and obedience." Stephen Olford

"Times of refreshing from the presence of the Lord." (Acts 3:19) J. Edwin Orr

"The awakening or quickening of God's people to their true nature and purpose." Robert Coleman

"The return of the Church from her backslidings, and the conversion of sinners." Charles Finney

"An extraordinary movement of the Holy Spirit producing extraordinary results." Richard Owen Roberts

"Revival is the church falling in love with Jesus all over again." Vance Havner

"The work of the Holy Spirit in restoring the people of God to a more vital spiritual life, witness, and work by prayer and the Word after repentance in crisis for their spiritual decline." Earle Cairns

The New Dictionary of Theology offers a helpful definition of revival: "God's quickening visitation of his people, touching their hearts and deepening his work of grace in their lives. It is essentially a corporate occurrence, an enlivening of individuals not in isolation but together."

Source: THE NEW DICTIONARY OF THEOLOGY

Revival, Religious: *This refers to staged episodes of increased religious emotion and group celebration, often to reclaim "sliding" religious commitment or moral values. Revivals are typically organized by established <u>religious groups</u>, and employ a variety of methods designed to arouse religious fervor. For examples of revivals, see <u>the First Great Awakening</u>, <u>the Second Great Awakening</u>, <u>Cane Ridge camp meeting</u>, and <u>Charles Finney's Rochester Revival</u>.*

Source: The Association of Religion Data Archives

GERALD L. PRIEST (1996, 225-226) DEFINES THE TERM "REVIVAL" AS FOLLOWS:

Revival is the noun form of the verb "revive," a derivation of the Latin re-vivere, meaning "to live again" or "to return or to restore to consciousness. Revival is the noun form of the verb "revive", a derivation of the Latin revivere, meaning "to live again" or "to return or to restore to consciousness or life." Revival can also be "the restoration of something to its true nature and purpose." Additionally, the term may mean "reform," as in the profound change of social morals or doctrine. It is in this sense we may understand the Protestant Reformation, for example. As we will see, the implication of the term scripturally and historically is that, while revival will result in moral reform, it is essentially a powerful work of the Holy Spirit in saving the lost and sanctifying the saved.

KAIROS - Evangelical Journal of Theology / Vol. VIII. No. 1 (2014), pp. 45-74

Bible Study and Personal Review Questions

1. On each of the numerous definitions and direct quotations presented here, ask the following search questions:
   a) What is the source of this quotation/definition?
   b) How exactly does it define and explain revival?
   c) What additional details does it add to the definition and explanation of revival presented at the beginning of this book?
   d) What impression does it give about God's revival as a universal need in the worldwide church of Christ?

CHAPTER TWO

SOME BIBLICAL PICTURES AND ILLUSTRATIONS OF REVIVAL TO MAKE IT UNDERSTANDABLE

<u>INTRODUCTION</u>

Even though revival can be explained with words as we have done in the previous chapter, because it is a human activity which also has a spiritual dimension, it can also be explained with both practical and biblical illustrations. These illustrations can then become word-pictures which will help us to understand what it is and what is actually involved in seeking God's revival. It is often said that one good picture or image is of more worth than a thousand words. What does this mean and what are its implications in writing and pedagogy? This statement is very true because we remember more what we see than what we read or hear. Though we have done our best to define and explain revival in the previous chapter it still stands to reason to present biblical pictures of this to help all our readers.

By way of illustration to emphasize this truth, a good teacher can teach everything he knows about the lion as an animal and describe it to the best of his ability with words. But if he wants to help his students to grasp all the details about the lion and remember his teachings throughout their lives, the best and the final thing to do will be his taking them to a zoo for them to look at a lion in its cage. When this is done, apart from giving the students a better understanding of all that the teacher has already said and taught them, this action will further help them to remember the lessons on the lion all through their lives. Though a good attempt has already been made to make revival understandable, we still believe that the best way to make revival fully comprehensible in this book is to present biblical pictures of it as we are going to try to do in this chapter with the following details:

I. THE REVIVAL OF ISRAEL IN THE VISION OF THE DRY BONES (Ezekiel 37:1-14)

Perhaps this picture is the most powerful illustration of spiritual revival in any church. Dry bones are bones with no muscles or tendons and can therefore be described as totally dry and dead with no hope of ever gaining life and becoming human again. Above all, the disjointed bones were haphazardly placed in the valley making it difficult to identify whose bone is this or whose bone is that. This compounded the impossibility of the revival and the resurrection. So if the prophecy revived and brought full life to these bones, then spiritual revival can be possible in any church no matter how dead it is.

The passage further indicates the source of the revival to us. First, it makes us aware that the great source of all revivals is God Himself who asked the question, "Can these bones live again?" Secondly, it reminds us that the great tool in the emergence of revival is the proclamation of God's unadulterated word. God's prophet spoke God's word exactly as given to him before life could come back to the dry bones. Thirdly, it reminds us that the power which works to effect and sustain every revival comes from the Holy Spirit. He brings the conviction of sin. He brings the repentance and confession. He brings the New Life and restoration and He works all the great miracles leading to spiritual elevation. This passage apart from the many lessons it offers us on revival in the church of Christ also offers us a good lesson that when we sincerely prepare the channels for revival to come, God will always grant it no matter how hopeless the situation of His people is.

This passage from Ezekiel 37:1-14 can be quoted and analyzed as follows to bring out its message and teaching on revival in the church of Christ today. It goes as follows:

<u>Ezekiel 37:1-14</u>
The hand of the Lord came upon me and brought me out in the Spirit of the Lord, and set me down in the midst of the valley; and it was full of bones. Then He caused me to pass by them all around, and behold, there were very many in the open valley; and indeed they were very dry. And He said to me, "Son of man,

can these bones live?" So I answered, "O Lord God, You know." Again He said to me, "Prophesy to these bones, and say to them, 'O dry bones, hear the word of the Lord! Thus says the Lord God to these bones: "Surely I will cause breath to enter into you, and you shall live. I will put sinews on you and bring flesh upon you, cover you with skin and put breath in you; and you shall live. Then you shall know that I am the Lord." ' "

So I prophesied as I was commanded; and as I prophesied, there was a noise, and suddenly a rattling; and the bones came together, bone to bone. Indeed, as I looked, the sinews and the flesh came upon them, and the skin covered them over; but there was no breath in them. Also He said to me, "Prophesy to the breath, prophesy, son of man, and say to the breath, 'Thus says the Lord God: "Come from the four winds, O breath, and breathe on these slain, that they may live." ' " So I prophesied as He commanded me, and breath came into them, and they lived, and stood upon their feet, an exceedingly great army.

Then He said to me, "Son of man, these bones are the whole house of Israel. They indeed say, Our bones are dry, our hope is lost, and we ourselves are cut off!' Therefore prophesy and say to them, 'Thus says the Lord God: "Behold, O My people, I will open your graves and cause you to come up from your graves, and bring you into the land of Israel. Then you shall know that I am the Lord, when I have opened your graves, O My people, and brought you up from your graves. I will put My Spirit in you, and you shall live, and I will place you in your own land. Then you shall know that I, the Lord, have spoken it and performed it," says the Lord.'" NKJV

As already mentioned, the valley of dry bones apart from being a pen portrait of the future revival of Israel, is also a perfect spiritual portrait of the possibility of God's mighty revivals in the Church of the Lord Jesus Christ today. This claim can be proved with the analysis of this passage as presented below:

1. The Valley of Dry Bones (Verse 1-3)
    This is a picture of the severe spiritual dryness we can experience in the church which will further remind us of the need for God's urgent revival.
2. Speaking life to the Dead Bones (Verse 4-6)

Revival from God is always possible in the Church if only we will sincerely desire it.

3. The Dead bones assemble together (Verse 7-8)

It is only the power of the Holy Spirit which is able to do the impossible to bring us revival.

4. The second prophecy to the bones bringing Life and Strength (Verse 9-10)

The new and vibrant life we are seeking in the church through revival can only come from God through His spirit.

5. God explaining the Vision to Ezekiel (Verse 11-14)

God has a message of hope, revival, renewal and restoration for the church today as He had for Israel.

II. THE PLAGUE OF SNAKES AND THE HOPE OF REVIVAL IN THE CHURCH TODAY

Another powerful picture illustration of revival in the church of the Lord Jesus Christ today is the picture of the brazing serpent God instructed Moses to mould and erect to bring healing and restoration to Israel after their disobedience. Let us start by reading this passage from Numbers 21:1-9.

<u>Numbers 21:1-9</u>

The king of Arad, the Canaanite, who dwelt in the South, heard that Israel was coming on the road to Atharim. Then he fought against Israel and took some of them prisoners. So Israel made a vow to the Lord, and said, "If You will indeed deliver this people into my hand, then I will utterly destroy their cities." And the Lord listened to the voice of Israel and delivered up the Canaanites, and they utterly destroyed them and their cities. So the name of that place was called Hormah.

Then they journeyed from Mount Hor by the Way of the Red Sea, to go around the land of Edom; and the soul of the people became very discouraged on the way. And the people spoke against God and against Moses: "Why have you brought us up out of Egypt to die in the wilderness? For there is no food and no water, and our soul loathes this worthless bread." So the Lord sent fiery serpents among the people, and they bit the people; and many of the people of Israel died.

Therefore the people came to Moses, and said, "We have sinned, for we have spoken against the Lord and against you; pray to the Lord that He take away the serpents from us." So Moses prayed for the people. Then the Lord said to Moses, "Make a fiery serpent, and set it on a pole; and it shall be that everyone who is bitten, when he looks at it, shall live." So Moses made a bronze serpent, and put it on a pole; and so it was, if a serpent had bitten anyone, when he looked at the bronze serpent, he lived. NKJV

There are four important pictures we can learn from this passage about revival in the church of Christ today. First, we can learn that when we initially come to the Lord with a good and committed heart and mind, we sense His powerful hands upon us to do us good, to bring us hope, to bring us resounding victories and for His presence to go before us as His chosen people. We read similar dealings with the Israelites at the beginning of the passage in the words, "So Israel made a vow to the Lord, and said, "If You will indeed deliver this people into my hand, then I will utterly destroy their cities." And the Lord listened iso the voice of Israel and delivered up the Canaanites, and they utterly destroyed them and their cities." This was a very good beginning for Israel in their walk with God. It was an attitude which brought God's full and powerful presence to be with them on all sides. One would have thought that they would have continued in this for a long time to maintain God's powerful hand upon them. But from nowhere, a sudden spiritual declension set in. What was it? It was the sin of murmuring and grumbling which leads us to the second lesson on revival in the passage.

The second lesson on Revival from this passage in the church of Christ today is that spiritual declension and degradation always comes as a result of sinfulness and rebellion resulting directly from backsliding and disobedience to God. This partly explains why there can never be any genuine revival without sincere repentance! What was the sin which led the Israelites to draw back from their holy, powerful and faithful God? Let us read it from the passage in the words, "And the people spoke against God and against Moses: "Why have you brought us up out of Egypt to die in the wilderness? For there is no food and no water, and our soul loathes this worthless bread." Can we expect such a statement from people who had miraculously crossed the red sea; who have been eating this well-balanced manna prepared from heaven without falling sick; who have been receiving a miraculous provision of shade by day and who have been receiving a miraculous provision of light and warmth every night in the form of a pillar of fire? But wait. Don't rush to criticize them because we are also like them in many respects in the church of the Lord Jesus Christ today.

Our God is holy and forever separated from evil. He can never live with sin in any form. So when the Israelites turned away from their righteous paths, what were the immediate results? The wrath of God came upon them immediately and fiery serpents entered their camp to cause their death. Sin, rebellion and worldliness have always been the cause of the spiritual death of believers in the church of Christ leading to spiritual decadence and the loss of the full operation of the Holy Spirit. This episode naturally leads us to the next great lesson on revival in the church of Christ today. What is this great lesson? It is that repentance is the key to revival. It is the key which opens the door to God's great room of mercy, forgiveness, pardon, cleansing, renewal and restoration. How did it happen in the case of the Israelites? And what lessons are available from it to us today in our quest for revival in the church of Christ?

This third lesson to us today on revival is simple and straight forward. **It is that, there is no revival without genuine repentance**! It is the repentance which will cause us to turn away from the sin and evil practices to help us avoid God's wrath and instead receive this forgiveness. If we are serious to get revival in the church of Christ today, let us learn a lesson on it from the Israelites in the passage. It reads as follows: "Therefore the people came to Moses, and said, "We have sinned, for we have spoken against the Lord and against you; pray to the Lord that He take away the serpents from us." So Moses prayed for the people. Then the

Lord said to Moses, "Make a fiery serpent, and set it on a pole; and it shall be that everyone who is bitten, when he looks at it, shall live." So Moses made a bronze serpent, and put it on a pole; and so it was, if a serpent had bitten anyone, when he looked at the bronze serpent, he lived."

From the serpents bite the people came to receive restoration and renewal which together form the fourth major lesson on revival in the church of the Lord Jesus Christ today – total renewal, restoration and spiritual empowerment to be able to forge ahead in Christ in new spiritual power and authority. But before this could take place, what immediately preceded it? It was sincere repentance and a return to God in sincere confession of sins for total forgiveness. Moses did not force them to come and repent. They themselves saw their waywardness and rebellion and rather went to God to confess for forgiveness. The result was God causing Moses to make a brazen serpent which became a source of their healing, restoration and resuscitation. Thus, we can also learn all the major issues involved in receiving God's revival in the church of the Lord Jesus Christ today from this great episode. Let us now move on to the next picture of revival in the Scriptures.

III. THE IMAGERY OF DROUGHT AND RAIN AND THE POSSIBILITY OF REVIVAL IN THE CHURCH OF CHRIST TODAY

Revival is often described in the Bible with the picture of God pouring abundant water on a dry and thirsty land. This reminds us that two metaphors which often appear in the Holy Bible in connection with the description of revival are spiritual dryness and abundance of rain water. Taking spiritual dryness first, we learn that it portrays the total lack of revival and spiritual vibrancy. Secondly the provision of abundant water through incessant rainfall is also given as a picture of God's spiritual revival. The first one which is often pictured as a lack of water on a dry land occurs because of prolonged drought in the midst of prolonged heat and sunshine. There are several Bible passages which talk about this as follows:

Psalm 68:6

God sets the solitary in families; He brings out those who are bound into prosperity; but the rebellious dwell in a dry land. NKJV

Psalm 63:1

O God, You are my God; early will I seek You; my soul thirsts for You; my flesh longs for You in a dry and thirsty land where there is no water. NKJV

Jeremiah 2:12-13

Be astonished, O heavens, at this, and be horribly afraid; be very desolate," says the Lord. "For My people have committed two evils: they have forsaken Me, the fountain of living waters, and hewn themselves cisterns — broken cisterns that can hold no water. NKJV

In all the passages quoted above, spiritual dryness which is the evidence of the lack of revival is described metaphorically as lack of water on a dry and thirsty land. We read this from Psalm 68:6 in the words: *"...but the rebellious dwell in a dry land." We also read it in Psalm 63:1 in the words: "...my soul thirsts for You; my flesh longs for You in a dry and thirsty land where there is no water."* Again it is emphasized in Jeremiah 2:13 in the words: *"…they have forsaken Me, the fountain of living waters, and hewn themselves cisterns – broken cisterns that can hold no water."* So in summary, when our spiritual fellowship with God breaks and we relapse into sin, spiritually we are pictured as a dry land with no water.

The second picture of revival which actually talks about the granting of revival by God in response to repentance and prayer is often described in the Bible with the provision of superabundance of rain and rainfall. Some of the Bible passages which use this figuratively can be discussed as follows:

Isaiah 44:3
For I will pour water on him who is thirsty, and floods on the dry ground; I will pour My Spirit on your descendants, and My blessing on your offspring. NKJV

Psalm 107:35
He turns a wilderness into pools of water, and dry land into watersprings. NKJV

When God promises and brings revival, this episode is described figuratively as His pouring of water (a symbol of the Holy Spirit) on a dry and parched land (a symbol of spiritually dehydrated believers). It is described in Isaiah 44:3 in the words: *"For I will pour water on him who is thirsty, and floods on the dry ground."* It is also highlighted in Psalm 107:35 in the words: *"He turns a wilderness into pools of water, and dry land into watersprings."* This means that revival is always possible if we are ready for it and are prepared to fulfil the conditions attached to it. These figures of drought and abundant rain are important in our discussion of the illustrations of revival because they do emphasize that through the normal human weaknesses and neglect, we can lose our spiritual fervour. But whenever this happens and we become like a dry and arid land spiritually, and we return to God in true penitence, He can pour His Spirit upon us abundantly like rainfall on dry ground to revive us.

All genuine revivals preceded by genuine repentance and a forsaking of all known sins always bring spiritual fruits and great and abundant blessings of revival which are often described with the imagery of fruitfulness, luxuriance and abundant growth which follow the continuous provision of rain after a long period of drought. Some of the Bible passages which use this figure of speech are as follows:

Hosea 10:12
Sow for yourselves righteousness; reap in mercy; break up your fallow ground, for it is time to seek the Lord, till He comes and rains righteousness on you. NKJV

Ezekiel 34:26-27
I will make them and the places all around My hill a blessing; and I will cause showers to come down in their season; there shall be showers of blessing. Then the trees of the field shall yield their fruit, and the earth shall yield her increase. They shall be safe in their land; and they shall know that I am the Lord, when I have broken the bands of their yoke and delivered them from the hand of those who enslaved them. NKJV

The blessings of revival as described in the two passages quoted above are described with the imagery of God pouring abundant spiritual blessings just like abundant rainfall which rainfall will bring them showers of blessings continually in a new fellowship and relationship with Him. In the passage quoted from Hosea 10:12 in the words: "for it is time to seek the Lord, till He comes and rains righteousness on you," God promises to pour righteousness like rain which is a major fruit of revival. In the reference quoted from the book of Ezekiel, the imagery of rainfall is still used in God's promise of what the passage calls showers of blessings. Showers of blessings are post-revival spiritual blessings which fall on God's people like rain showers.

To conclude this discussion, we want to emphasize that because God has used common everyday things around us like drought, rainfall, dry and parched land and abundance of water to describe both spiritual dryness and spiritual abundance, it should not be difficult for us to understand the subject of revival at all.

We have all been thirsty before and know what water does in such situations in practical terms. When this is applied to any spiritual situation, it must be readily understood. Let us finish off our discussion of spiritual dryness and spiritual abundance with some of the words of this great hymn often sung in the church of Christ in connection with God's abundant spiritual provisions, spiritual luxuriance and special spiritual blessings.

1

There shall be showers of blessing:

This is the promise of love;

There shall be seasons refreshing,

Sent from the Savior above.

Showers of blessing,

Showers of blessing we need;

Mercy-drops round us are falling,

But for the showers we plead.

2.

There shall be showers of blessing –

Precious reviving again;

Over the hills and the valleys,

Sound of abundance of rain.

Category: Fullness of the Spirit

Lyrics: Daniel Webster Whittle (1840-1901)

Music: James McGranahan (1840-1907)

Let us now turn to the next illustration of revival which is the transfiguration of the Lord Jesus Christ.

IV. THE TRANSFIGURATION OF CHRIST AS A PICTURE OF GOD'S REVIVAL

The transfiguration of Christ can be read in the following passages in the gospels:

Matthew 17:1-9; Mark 9:2-9; Luke 9:28-36. Let us quote and read the reference from Matthew 17:1-9 as follows:

Matthew 17:1-9

After six days Jesus took with him Peter, James and John the brother of James, and led them up a high mountain by themselves. There he was transfigured before them. His face shone like the sun, and his clothes became as white as the light. Just then there appeared before them Moses and Elijah, talking with Jesus. Peter said to Jesus, "Lord, it is good for us to be here. If you wish, I will put up three shelters – one for you, one for Moses and one for Elijah." While he was still speaking, a bright cloud covered them, and a voice from the cloud said, "This is my Son, whom I love; with him I am well pleased. Listen to him!" When the disciples heard this, they fell facedown to the ground, terrified. But Jesus came and touched them. "Get up," he said. "Don't be afraid." When they looked up, they saw no one except Jesus. As they were coming down the mountain, Jesus instructed them, "Don't tell anyone what you have seen, until the Son of Man has been raised from the dead." NIV

Another important picture of revival granted to us in the Bible is the Transfiguration of the Lord Jesus in the presence of His disciples on the mountain. When this great event took place, it was a great manifestation of God's revival because it brought down God's special presence for Him to speak directly and audibly to everybody's hearing. In all situations of revival, the transformation, renewal and restoration we receive is as the direct result of the special presence of God which comes down to His faithful and spiritually thirsty children. This great episode should teach us the following truths about God's revival.

First, that revival can come to us only from our true and powerful God. As we pray for revival, our focus must be upon the mercy and grace of our omnipotent God because He is the true source of all revivals which come only by the manifestation of His powerful presence as it occurred on the mountain.

Secondly, we must also learn this truth about God's revival that it is granted only when we have prepared to mount in prayer as Jesus and these disciples went up on this high mountain to pray. In seeking true revival, we should always find time to pray fervently after initially repenting of our sins for cleansing in the blood of Christ. This is the only way to make a special visitation of the holy God possible.

Thirdly, we must always expect great things from God anytime we dedicate ourselves to prayer for God's revival. Great things happened on the Day of Pentecost when God's revival came down. Similarly, great things occurred during God's visitation on the mountain. God's voice was clearly heard by all. His glory also became visible to all. The attestation of Jesus as the only Messiah and saviour of the world was also heard by all and there was great joy and a high spiritual elevation. It is this great and powerful presence of God which always brings down His revival to us in the Church. What can we also do in our local churches today to bring down God's revival learning from what took place on the mountain at the Transfiguration? It was no wonder they were not prepared to come down but to remain there forever because of the joy of God's presence.

Let us conclude our discussion of the biblical pictures and illustrations of revival in this chapter by looking at what happened on the day of Pentecost.

V. THE FIRST GREAT REVIVAL OF THE NEW TESTAMENT ON THE DAY OF PENTECOST

One of the best pictures and illustrations of revival in the church today is the revival which occurred in Jerusalem on the Day of Pentecost. It has had a great all-time relevance to the church and its continuous ministries throughout all the ages to the present day. Today, it still offers us some important and essential lessons on God's revivals. If we really want to understand the concept of revival, renewal and restoration in the New Testament Church and further learn lessons on how to seek God's revival constantly in the universal Church of Christ, then it should be our great reference point. Some of its precious lessons on revivals which we want to discuss here can be outlined as follows:

First, it tells us that revivals are always born as a result of intense continuous and corporate prayer. Secondly, it tells us that it is God who always grants revivals by His Spirit when we prepare the ground for it. Thirdly, it makes us aware that whenever and wherever genuine revivals occur, they bring a great social and spiritual impact. Finally, it emphasizes that if we want the church of Christ to advance by leaps and bounds, then we should make time to seek and maintain God's constant revival. Let us discuss this picture of revival on the Day of Pentecost plus its lessons one by one starting with the appropriate biblical passages which describe this great spiritual event:

Acts 2:1-4

When the Day of Pentecost had fully come, they were all with one accord in one place. And suddenly there came a sound from heaven, as of a rushing mighty wind, and it filled the whole house where they were sitting. Then there appeared to them divided tongues, as of fire, and one sat upon each of them. And they were all filled with the Holy Spirit and began to speak with other tongues, as the Spirit gave them utterance. NKJV

The first great lesson offered to us on revivals in the church by the first revival on the Day of Pentecost is obedience. Obedience is compliance with an order or instruction which demonstrates total submission to a higher authority. Why are we saying that the whole event which occurred on the Day of Pentecost is a direct result of total obedience? It is because the actual beginning of the Day of Pentecost is embedded in Luke 24:49 which reads: "Behold, I send the Promise of My Father upon you; but tarry in the city of Jerusalem until you are endued with power from on high." It was in obedience to this instruction from Christ which was given before His ascension that we got the Day of Pentecost. The believers gathered to pray in the upper room because Christ had instructed them to remain in Jerusalem for some unspecified number of days until the Spirit of God brings them power from on high to be able to do the work of God. They gathered in Jerusalem to pray because they desired this power. The lesson here is clear. Revival can come to us wherever we are in the Church of Christ today only when we desire it.

A second great lesson we can learn from this episode on revivals is the matter of prayer and patient waiting. Prayer has and will always be the key which opens the door to God's treasure house of power, revival and renewal. The feast of Pentecost always occurred some 50 days after the Passover. That this event took place on the Day of Pentecost presupposes that the believers went into hiding to pray as Christ had commanded them some time after the Passover and continued in prayer for many days before this revival occurred. The great lesson here on revivals in the church is that we can never receive any continuous revivals until we first learn to be continuous in prayer as the disciples and the early believers did.

A third great lesson on revivals from the Day of Pentecost which is still of great relevance in the Church of Christ today is the truth that spiritual revivals are always centered on God's power. It is God's power which descends upon us both as individuals and as a church to bring us great empowerment and special enablement to do whatever God has planned to use us for. It was this power which gave God's people the supernatural utterance to be able to speak in languages they had never learnt before to enable them to share the gospel with the many pilgrims who had gathered in Jerusalem from different parts of the then known world. When we are fully revived and fully backed by God's power through continuous revivals, we can do in one week what will take us one year or more to do.

A final lesson we can learn from this great awakening on revivals is that whenever they occur, though they start in the temple or church building, they do not remain there but come out to impact people's lives and to bring them some of the fruits of revival like salvation, healing, deliverance and hope in the community at large. What happened on the Day of Pentecost is a perfect portrait and picture of the type of revival Christ wants to see regularly in His Church from Pentecost to the rapture. Let us study it regularly as an illustration of revivals in the church of Christ.

PART 2

UNDERSTANDING GOD'S PERSONAL REVIVALS FOR THE INDIVIDUAL CHRISTIAN

PREAMBLE

Whenever the word "Revival" is mentioned in the church, many people often think of it only in terms of big revival services like mini and mega revivals. There is nothing wrong with this. It is normal whenever revival is being sought at the general church level through the normal mini and mega revival services.

But apart from seeking God's revivals at the general church level together with other believers, it must also be emphasied and clearly understood that regular revivals can also be sought at the *personal induvial level as **PERSONAL REVIVALS*** either as a compliment to what we receive at the general church level, or as a replacement for what we should have got in the church but which is not forthcoming for some reasons.

Personal Revivals are the second great avenue to seek and obtain regular spiritual renewals and spiritual revitalizations. The advantages of maintaining a regular personal revival program are numerous and include the following. First, you are able to seek, obtain, and maintain God's regular spiritual renewals at the personal whether the church organises regular revival services or not. Secondly, if your church organises mini and mega revival services regularly, they help you to keep your revival fire burning in between these programs. Thirdly, they provide you with the opportunity to check and remove all traces of spiritual backsliding and spiritual declension before they gain any firm hold upon you.

So understanding personal revival and knowing how to seek it regularly is equally as important as going through the general revival programs of the church. In churches where these revival services are regularly held, they can become a useful supplement. In churches where these regular revival services are non-existent, they can provide a useful replacement. Let us try to discover all the essential facts about seeking personal revivals in the next two chapters with the following details:

CHAPTER THREE

UNDERSTANDING AND SEEKING GOD'S PERSONAL REVIVAL REGULARLY (PART 1)

INTRODUCTION

There are two major ways revivals can occur in the life of the local Church. First, such revivals can occur at the personal level. This means the revivals will begin and spread in the church from person to person until it bursts into a mighty holy flame to engulf the whole church. In fact, most revivals as depicted in the history of the church came into the Church of Christ this way. Secondly, revivals can also begin at the general church level when the local church leadership understands the importance of regular revivals and initiates mini and mega revival programmes to promote it from time to time. But it must be quickly pointed out that whether revivals start from the personal level or from the general church level, the spiritual and practical principles which cause it to come down from heaven are always the same.

Because of the ignorance many church members harbour about personal revivals, whenever the word revival is mentioned in the church, we think only about group revivals at the general church level. This further leads them to adopt a wrong attitude towards revival by their looking at the head of the church, their local pastors and other church leaders to throw it down to them like a parcel. But this is absolutely wrong! These leaders can provide the guidance in the form of teaching, and further provide other types of support in the search for revival. But the actual task of working to bring down the revival is the task of the Holy Spirit but which practically involves everybody in the local church including both the church members and the local church leadership.

When the local church members come to understand personal revivals very well, even if some church leaders initially do not see the need for any revival in the local church, God's revival can still start at the personal, individual and family levels and spread from these faithful sources to affect the whole church. Such faithful individuals and families can thereby be the channels and vessels for God's revival in the church from where God's unquenchable flames of revival can start and soon catch up with the whole church. It is for this reason that we want to discuss personal revivals in this and the next chapter of this book together with the corporate ones as already defined in chapter 1 of this book to help everybody in the church who desires God's revival to be able to maintain the balance between personal and group revivals. Let us now proceed with the details:

THE DEFINITION AND EXPLANATION OF PERSONAL REVIVAL

<u>INTRODUCTION</u>

Personal revival is the genesis of all true revivals in the church of Christ. The explanation for this can be found in the fact that all true revivals initially begin as personal revivals with the individual Christians forming the church before becoming corporate revivals spreading to affect all persons in the church when these individually revived children of God come together as the local body of believers at the general church level to share fellowship. In fact, there can never be any corporate revivals without the foundational personal revivals just as there can never be any rains without clouds.

So seeking to understand personal revival at the very beginning of a book like this is of vital importance to the whole question of revivals. This is so because in doing this we are touching the very roots of the revivals being sought apart from laying a solid foundation for any anticipated revivals to occur. It is for this reason that we have taken great pains to define and explain personal revivals thoroughly as we have done below with all the important and necessary essentials.

To fully amplify the meaning of personal revivals to incorporate all the necessary details, we have tried to define and explain personal revivals from three different angels. These explanations follow this order:

Definition 1
Personal revival can be defined as the consciousness which comes to a person or individual to seek and become fully awakened and

alive spiritually. It can further be described as a great personal spiritual revitalization or renewal which manifests practically in daily life after starting spiritually.

Definition 2

Personal revival can be defined as the deep spiritual renewal and spiritual resuscitation which is sought and received by zealous and sincere Christians and which is always followed by a decisive practical change manifesting in activities like those listed below:

i. Immediate turning away from sin through genuine repentance.

    ### Acts 3:19
    Repent therefore and be converted, that your sins may be blotted out, so that times of refreshing may come from the presence of the Lord. NKJV

ii. Faithful confession of all known sins for cleansing by the blood of Jesus

    ### 1 John 1:9
    If we confess our sins, He is faithful and just to forgive us our sins and to cleanse us from all unrighteousness. NKJV

iii. Removal of grudge and bitterness from the heart through the forgiveness of all the persons who have offended and hurt you.

<u>Matthew 5:23, 24</u>
Therefore if you bring your gift to the altar, and there remember that your brother has something against you, leave your gift there before the altar, and go your way. First be reconciled to your brother, and then come and offer your gift. NKJV

iv. Approaching and seeking forgiveness from people you have also hurt and offended you

<u>Matthew 6:14, 15</u>
For if ye forgive men their trespasses, your heavenly Father will also forgive you: But if ye forgive not men their trespasses, neither will your Father forgive your trespasses. KJV

v. Making amends and practical restitution to God and other human personalities such as sending back and restoring their stolen items and other practical demonstrations of making amends.

<u>Luke 19:8</u>
Then Zacchaeus stood and said to the Lord, "Look, Lord, I give half of my goods to the poor; and if I have

taken anything from anyone by false accusation, I restore fourfold." NKJV

vi. Seeking to walk in the former New Life available in Christ in the light of 2 Corinthians 5:17 which says, *"Therefore, if anyone is in Christ, he is a new creation; old things have passed away; behold, all things have become new."* NKJV

vii. Seeking to pattern your life in total obedience to God's word and to the promptings of the Holy Spirit.

Galatians 5:16

I say then: Walk in the Spirit, and you shall not fulfill the lust of the flesh. NKJV

viii. Publicly sharing the gospel with boldness with your neighbours and family members.

Romans 15:19, 20

In mighty signs and wonders, by the power of the Spirit of God, so that from Jerusalem and round about to Illyricum I have fully preached the gospel of Christ. And so I have made it my aim to preach the gospel, not where Christ was named, lest I should build on another man's foundation. NKJV

Definition 3

Personal revivals are personal spiritual renewals, spiritual freshness and spiritual restorations sought earnestly by faith from the Holy Spirit and granted with amazing and beneficial spiritual results in the lives of the individual seekers. Whenever it truly takes place, its practical results are so deep seated that they bring far-reaching spiritual transformation which affects the totality of the individual seekers in some of the important areas of life such as are listed below as follows:

i. Personal revival leads to a new thirst and hunger for God as well as all His spiritual values.

Psalm 42:1, 2
As the deer pants for the water brooks, So pants my soul for You, O God. My soul thirsts for God, for the living God. When shall I come and appear before God? NKJV

Matthew 5:6
Blessed are those who hunger and thirst for righteousness, for they shall be filled. NKJV

ii.   Personal revival rekindles the fire of God and the fire of the Holy Spirit in our spiritual lives for us to be ablaze for God once again.

<u>2 Timothy 1:6-7</u>
Therefore I remind you to stir up the gift of God which is in you through the laying on of my hands. For God has not given us a spirit of fear, but of power and of love and of a sound mind. NKJV

<u>Acts 2:3</u>
Then there appeared to them divided tongues, as of fire, and one sat upon each of them. NKJV

iii.   Personal revivals renew our spiritual peace and joy in Christ.

<u>Galatians 5:22</u>
But the fruit of the Spirit is love, joy, peace, longsuffering, kindness, goodness, faithfulness. NKJV

<u>John 16:24</u>
Until now you have asked nothing in My name. Ask, and you will receive, that your joy may be full. NKJV

iv. Personal revival renews our passion for God and His work to share the gospel regularly with sinners.

<u>1 Corinthians 15:58</u>
Therefore, my beloved brethren, be steadfast, immovable, always abounding in the work of the Lord, knowing that your labor is not in vain in the Lord. NKJV

<u>Ecclesiastes 9:10</u>
Whatever your hand finds to do, do it with your might; for there is no work or device or knowledge or wisdom in the grave where you are going. (change version to. NIV

v. Personal revival restores God's full and manifest presence in our lives.

<u>Exodus 33:14</u>
And He said, "My Presence will go with you, and I will give you rest."

vi. Personal revival restores our first love for Christ.

<u>Revelation 2:4-5</u>

Nevertheless I have this against you, that you have left your first love. Remember therefore from where you have fallen; repent and do the first works, or else I will come to you quickly and remove your lampstand from its place – unless you repent. NKJV

vii. Personal revival brings us a deep spiritual enlightenment and a deep sense of God and Christ.

<u>1 Corinthians 2:10</u>
But God has revealed them to us through His Spirit. For the Spirit searches all things, yes, the deep things of God. NKJV

<u>1 Corinthians 14:20</u>
Brethren, do not be children in understanding; however, in malice be babes, but in understanding be mature. NKJV

viii. Personal revival instills holiness and spiritual purity in us in our daily walk.

<u>Hebrews 12:14</u>
Pursue peace with all people, and holiness, without which no one will see the Lord. NKJV

<u>Galatians 5:16</u>

I say then: Walk in the Spirit, and you shall not fulfill the lust of the flesh. NKJV

1 Peter 1:15, 16

But as He who called you is holy, you also be holy in all your conduct, because it is written, "Be holy, for I am holy." NKJV

ix.   Personal revival restores our standing as genuine children of God to us.

1 Corinthians 16:13

Watch, stand fast in the faith, be brave, be strong. NKJV

Philippians 2:14, 15

Do all things without complaining and disputing, that you may become blameless and harmless, children of God without fault in the midst of a crooked and perverse generation, among whom you shine as lights in the world. NKJV

x.   Personal revival ensures our steady spiritual progress from one degree of glory into another.

Psalm 92:12

The righteous shall flourish like a palm tree, he shall grow like a cedar in Lebanon. NKJV

<u>2 Corinthians 3:18</u>

But we all, with unveiled face, beholding as in a mirror the glory of the Lord, are being transformed into the same image from glory to glory, just as by the Spirit of the Lord. NKJV

xi. Personal revival opens the door of God's spiritual blessings to us.

<u>Matthew 6:33</u>

But seek first the kingdom of God and His righteousness, and all these things shall be added to you. NKJV

xii. Personal revival opens the door of God's material blessings to us.
<u>Ecclesiastes 5:19</u>

As for every man to whom God has given riches and wealth, and given him power to eat of it, to receive his heritage and rejoice in his labor – this is the gift of God. NKJV

xiii. Personal revival ensures our moving from grace to grace daily to be able to continue the Christian race.

<u>2 Peter 3:18</u>

But grow in the grace and knowledge of our Lord and Savior Jesus Christ. To Him be the glory both now and forever. Amen. NKJV

1 Peter 5:10
But may the God of all grace, who called us to His eternal glory by Christ Jesus, after you have suffered a while, perfect, establish, strengthen, and settle you. NKJV

xiv.   Personal revival always helps us to remain spiritually fresh and vibrant in the Lord.

Romans 12:11, 12
Not lagging in diligence, fervent in spirit, serving the Lord; rejoicing in hope, patient in tribulation, continuing steadfastly in prayer. NKJV

xv.   Personal revival ensures our access to God's throne of grace always.

Hebrews 4:16
Let us therefore come boldly to the throne of grace, that we may obtain mercy and find grace to help in time of need. NKJV

xvi.   Personal revival brings us spiritual rebirth and spiritual restoration like in the valley of Dry bones. (quote relevant portion from valley of the dry bones; ref: someone born of the spirit is like the air – words from Jesus to Nicodemus)

<u>Ezekiel 37:1, 2</u>
The hand of the Lord came upon me and brought me out in the Spirit of the Lord, and set me down in the midst of the valley; and it was full of bones. Then He caused me to pass by them all around, and behold, there were very many in the open valley; and indeed they were very dry. NKJV

<u>Ezekiel 37:10</u>
So I prophesied as He commanded me, and breath came into them, and they lived, and stood upon their feet, an exceedingly great army. NKJV

xvii.   Personal revival changes our spiritual identity from spiritual coldness and sinfulness to spiritual rebirth and newness of life.

<u>Revelation 3:15, 16</u>
"I know your works, that you are neither cold nor hot. I could wish you were cold or hot. So then, because you are lukewarm, and neither cold nor hot, I will vomit you out of My mouth. NKJV

<u>Acts 4:31</u>

And when they had prayed, the place where they were assembled together was shaken; and they were all filled with the Holy Spirit, and they spoke the word of God with boldness. NKJV

xviii. Personal revival leads to a drastic change in our spiritual status, drawing a line between the past life of spiritual failure and the present life of spiritual victory.

Romans 12:2

And do not be conformed to this world, but be transformed by the renewing of your mind, that you may prove what is that good and acceptable and perfect will of God. NKJV

2 Corinthians 5:17

Therefore, if anyone is in Christ, he is a new creation; old things have passed away; behold, all things have become new. NKJV

xix. Personal revival is comparable to the refueling and recharging of our personal spiritual lives to be able to press on in the Christian journey with greater victory than before.

Philippians 3:14

I press toward the goal for the prize of the upward call of God in Christ Jesus.

Isaiah 40:31

But those who wait on the Lord shall renew their strength; they shall mount up with wings like eagles, they shall run and not be weary, They shall walk and not faint. NKJV

Lamentations 3:25, 26

The Lord is good to those who wait for Him, To the soul who seeks Him. It is good that one should hope and wait quietly for the salvation of the Lord. NKJV

CONCLUSION

Before we end this discussion on the definition and explanation of personal revivals, we want to sum up all the important personal, spiritual and practical traits of such personally revived persons as follows:

1. All such personally revived persons are people "caused to live again" as fully renewed individuals to the glory of God.

2. Consequently, they live as people upon whom God can fully rely spiritually to help build His church.

3. Their renewed and restored lives become a source of inspiration which pose a great challenge to all those around them in the communities in which they are.

4. Ultimately, they get the necessary divine strength to be able to live as people who are fully empowered by the Holy Spirit to get involved in active service for Christ.

THE ENCOURAGEMENT TO SEEK PERSONAL REVIVAL

Because of its importance to our survival as Christians, the Bible constantly encourages us to seek personal revival using various figures of speech. Classic examples of these encouragements are as follows:

I. Breaking Our Unplowed or Fallow Ground
<u>Hosea 10:12</u>

Sow for yourselves righteousness; Reap in mercy; Break up your fallow ground, For it is time to seek the Lord, Till He comes and rains righteousness on you. NKJV

Fallow ground is a field which has been left uncultivated for a long time. So breaking your fallow ground means going to plow and cultivate this land for it to be useful. So to the Christian breaking your fallow ground means opening up and confessing the sins we thought we could hide from God. This practically involves being open about our secret sins and all sins touching on vulnerability, honesty, accountability and morality. Being ready to break our fallow ground obliges us to confront these sins that appear to be familiar and comfortable to us but which are the sins which cause our spiritual death and degradation. Breaking our fallow ground helps us to admit that the sins which have become idols to us can be admitted, confessed and completely forsaken to bring us revival, spiritual renewal and spiritual restoration. Are you prepared to break your fallow ground today as you read this book?

II. Uprooting the Thorns and Thistles
Jeremiah 4:3, 4

For thus says the Lord to the men of Judah and Jerusalem: "Break up your fallow ground, and do not sow among thorns. Circumcise yourselves to the Lord, and take away the foreskins of your hearts, you men of Judah and inhabitants of Jerusalem, lest My fury come forth like fire, and burn so that no one can quench it, because of the evil of your doings." NKJV

Thorns and thistles in agricultural practice are useless weeds which kill good and useful crops which can be used as food. So before you can sow any such good crops, the thorns and thistles occupying the land must first be uprooted. In this, the thorns and thistles become comparable to the sins which choke and kill our spiritual lives and bring us into a state of spiritual dullness and total spiritual death. So before we can receive God's revival, all the spiritual thorns and thistles in our lives must be removed to bring the fresh activity of the Holy Spirit into our spiritual lives to revive us.

To us as Christians, a great spiritual lesson for us is that without the continuous revival, renewal and refreshing of the Holy Spirit in continuous spiritual reawakening, we can become weeds, thistles, thorns and tares as human beings. We therefore constantly need to drink deeply from the word of God and pray without ceasing so as not to quench the power of God in our daily lives to become cold Christians. So these two metaphors are a great encouragement to us to seek and maintain God's personal revival in our lives.

III. Encouragement to Sow Righteousness and Truth as the Seeds of Personal Revival

It is important to note that in the metaphor of the fallow ground and that of the thorns and thistles, the cultivation of righteousness is mentioned together with these imageries. Hosea 10:12 says, "Sow for yourselves righteousness" and Jeremiah 4:4a says, "Circumcise yourselves to the Lord, and take away the foreskins of your hearts." Both passages are calls to righteousness which should go with the call for revival and spiritual renewal as discussed above. This in effect means that after we have removed the thorns from our lives as an ongoing process, we also need to sow seeds of righteousness and truth constantly to be able to receive, maintain and stay in God's personal revival.

This involves renewing our commitment to biblical truth and more importantly living to be practical testimonies of the truth and purity taught by Christ to be upheld and followed by all His genuine disciples and followers. This is the truth which has been emphasized with the imagery of the fallow ground and in the metaphor of uprooting our thorns and thistles. With these pictures, the Holy Spirit is giving us all the encouragement to seek personal revival constantly as we continue to run the Christian race so that we can neither falter nor become discouraged in the Christian race but will surely finish this race in the strength and power of the Holy Spirit.

KNOWING SOME OF THE IMPORTANT PRACTICAL ISSUES INVOLVED IN SEEKING REGULAR PERSONAL REVIVALS

Personal revivals are not different from group revivals in terms of practice and mode of attainment and the spiritual and practical benefits which can accrue from them. This means by implication that the same things we do at the general church level to receive it are the same things we do at the personal level to be able to receive it; and the same benefits which come to us when we become personally revived, are the same gains which we attain in the group revival at the general church level. So in this section, we want to discuss some of the essential things we should check in our lives regularly to be able to stay revived at the personal level. To help us do this biblically and appropriately, we want to mention specifically some of the spiritual and practical things we should check constantly to be able to receive and maintain God's personal revival all the time.

Everything in God's creative order runs and works on some form of strength, energy and power. This is true both in the spiritual and practical sense. In this way, the success of any major spiritual or physical undertaking is largely dependent upon the strength, power and energy behind it. If we can receive God's personal revival regularly and maintain it to our spiritual advantage permanently, then this greatly depends upon the spiritual power backing us which can be obtained from the sources mentioned and discussed below with the following details:

I. WE SHOULD CONSTANTLY CHECK OUR PRAYER AND DEVOTIONAL LIFE

1. We should endeavour to pray without season.
   <u>1 Thessalonians 5:17</u>
   pray without ceasing.
2. We should do our best to Study and apply the Word of God regularly and daily
3. We should always be attentive to the voice of the Holy Spirit.
4. We should avoid all hindrances to revival in our lives.
5. We must desire and be prepared to pay the price to receive God's revival all the time.
6. We must be prepared to do the things which can help us to mount spiritually all the time.

A vibrant and a sustainable prayer and devotional life is an invaluable asset to our acquiring and walking in God's revival throughout our Christian lives. The reasons are not hard to find. But let us simply start by stating that your daily prayer and devotional life and how vigilant you are as a Christian is important. It is like the engine which powers a car or the battery which powers the electrical system of your car or mobile phone. When the battery or engine power goes down, there is no way you can get optimum performance from your vehicle, phone or other essential gadgets.

The daily devotional life of every true Christian who claims to have been personally revived must be strong and vibrant as a genuine indicator of his spirituality and true spiritual level. This is needed to help him in his daily spiritual victory and survival. By way of comparison, when your phone power reaches the lowest level of power it will automatically shut down. As a Christian, the source of your power which strengthens you daily is your devotional prayer, devotional Bible study and devotional fellowship with Christ, God and the Holy Spirit. So very often the failure of our daily devotional life incorporating all the essential items mentioned above is the beginning of the loss of our personal power and personal revival and the first major step toward spiritual backsliding. So check your daily devotional life to be able to pray and study God's word constantly to pave the way for you to be able to receive and maintain your personal revival all the time.

II. WE SHOULD CONSTANTLY CHECK OUR SECRET LIFE REGULARLY TO AVOID HYPOCRISY

- What is a hypocritical life? Hypocrisy is feigning to be what you are not or creating a public impression that you have attained what in actual fact you don't have. A life of hypocrisy can lead you to claim to have been personally revived when in practice, you are not bearing any of the marks of a personally revived person. Examples of hypocrisy in the Bible can be found in the lives of the following people:

<u>Mark 7:6</u>

He replied, "Isaiah was right when he prophesied about you hypocrites; as it is written: "'These people honor me with their lips, but their hearts are far from me. NIV

Titus 1:16

They profess to know God, but in works they deny Him, being abominable, disobedient, and disqualified for every good work. NKJV

Matthew 23:27-28

"Woe to you, scribes and Pharisees, hypocrites! For you are like whitewashed tombs which indeed appear beautiful outwardly, but inside are full of dead men's bones and all uncleanness. Even so you also outwardly appear righteous to men, but inside you are full of hypocrisy and lawlessness. NKJV

Check whether you are in secret what you are in public. Hypocrisy can kill your advancement in personal revival.

One major area where a lot of believers exhibit great hypocrisy to kill their personal revival is in the area of Christian holiness and morality. A lot of Christians always create the false impression that they are living for Christ in holiness, purity and sanctification in their daily practical lives when this is not the case. This is especially true in the area of immorality in general resulting in fornication, adultery and all the known sexual deviations can never grant personal revival where such acts of sexual immorality are rife but hypocritically conceived. A life which is personally revived can quickly lose this revival through these shameful acts of sexual immorality.

<u>1 John 2:15</u>
Do not love the world or the things in the world. If anyone loves the world, the love of the Father is not in him. NKJV

<u>1 Thessalonians 4:3</u>
For this is the will of God, your sanctification: that you should abstain from sexual immorality. NKJV

III. WE SHOULD CONSTANTLY CHECK OUR PRACTICAL LIVES TO AVOID COMPROMISE

- What does it mean to be a compromising Christian? It means to weaken your Christian principles and make them less strong and firm; or weaken your standards and morals as a Christian to be drawn into sin and to do things which are contrary to God's plan and will for your life.

- Compromise leading to disobedience caused the fall of King Solomon. (Deuteronomy 17:17 with 1 kings 11:3)

Deuteronomy 17:17
Neither shall he multiply wives for himself, lest his heart turn away; nor shall he greatly multiply silver and gold for himself.

1 Kings 11:3
And he had seven hundred wives, princesses, and three hundred concubines; and his wives turned away his heart.

The great danger about compromise in all situations is that it causes us to lose our spiritual commitment to Christ which is one of the main preconditions for revival. By definition, the truly committed Christian is that person who exhibits unflinching devotion to Christ and to all his Christian principles in the face of challenges, very serious temptations to compromise and to abandon his faith. When your commitment level starts going down because of gradual compromise like King Solomon, then know that you can soon lose your personal revival and land in big spiritual trouble and confusion.

IV. *WE SHOULD CONSTANTLY CHECK OUR LACK OF ZEAL FOR GOD'S WORK*

- Zeal is personal eagerness and strong interest in doing something. To the Christian and in relation to God's work, it is the strong eagerness, interest and enthusiasm we have for God and service in His vineyard. Zeal is one strong proof of personal revival. Examples of holy zeal for God in the Bible are as follows:

1 Kings 19:9-10

And there he went into a cave, and spent the night in that place; and behold, the word of the Lord came to him, and He said to him, "What are you doing here, Elijah?" So he said, "I have been very zealous for the Lord God of hosts; for the children of Israel have forsaken Your covenant, torn down Your altars, and killed Your prophets with the sword. I alone am left; and they seek to take my life." NKJV

Romans 12:11

Not lagging in diligence, fervent in spirit, serving the Lord. NKJV

Though zeal is an inner urge to stand for God and His cause with great strength and enthusiasm, whenever and wherever it works, it is exhibited in practical action not only to stand for God but also to work for Him with great faithfulness. This was what Elijah did during his time and this is the exact thing we are also being encouraged to do in the passage quoted in Romans 12:11.

V. WE SHOULD CONSTANTLY CHECK OUR SPIRITUAL POWER LEVEL

Personal revival like group revivals always brings down the power of God upon those who are personally revived. Apart from equipping such saints for active and successful Christian service, this power also bears testimony to the fact that God's revival fire is still burning in the life of the individual Christian.

Acts 1:8

But you shall receive power when the Holy Spirit has come upon you; and you shall be witnesses to Me in Jerusalem, and in all Judea and Samaria, and to the end of the earth." NKJV

Acts 4:31

And when they had prayed, the place where they were assembled together was shaken; and they were all filled with the Holy Spirit, and they spoke the word of God with boldness. NKJV

Ephesians 5:18

"And do not be drunk with wine, in which is dissipation; but be filled with the Spirit." NKJV

Do you sense the fullness of the Spirit in your life? Do you sense the power of the Holy Spirit in your life? Whenever you sense that the power of God is no more upon you as it used to be, that is the time to seek personal infilling to renew your life of personal revival to be able to avoid the tendency to hypocrisy, compromise and loss of zeal which can draw you into total backsliding. Even after the great day of Pentecost, the disciples and Apostles constantly sought fresh infillings of the Holy Spirit to be able to persevere in the work of Christ. If we can maintain our personal revival today, then we should never gloss over Ephesians 5:18 even in a day.

VI. *WE SHOULD CONSTANTLY CHECK OUR RELATIONSHIP WITH THE WORLD AND OUR INVOLVEMENT IN WORLDLINESS*

Anybody who is personally revived by the Holy Spirit lives and walks in the truth of James 4:4 which says: "Adulterers and adulteresses! Whoever therefore wants to be a friend of the world makes himself an enemy of God." Do you not know that friendship with the world is enmity with God? What is worldliness according to 1 John 2:15-17. What type of life can be termed as worldly? In fact, worldliness and friendship with the world have always been some of the major enemies of personal revival. If this temptation to worldliness is checked regularly, we can constantly be revived by the Holy Spirit and always stay revived.

<u>1 John 2:15-17</u>
Do not love the world or the things in the world. If anyone loves the world, the love of the Father is not in him. For all that is in the world — the lust of the flesh, the lust of the eyes, and the pride of life — is not of the Father but is of the world. And the world is passing away, and the lust of it; but he who does the will of God abides forever. NKJV

CONCLUSION

Whenever we sense any of these symptoms which can lead to the loss of our personal revival, then we should start seeking biblical remedies before any spiritual degradation sets in. Some of these spiritual remedies can be outlined as follows:

Remedy 1

We should go on our knees immediately and confess these spiritual weaknesses and cracks as King David did.

Remedy 2

We should be bold and specific to pray for immediate spiritual restoration and ask the Lord for spiritual reparation and reawakening by emulating saints like King David, the Apostle Peter and many others who through their penitence could walk successfully with the Lord up to the end.

Remedy 3

This is also the time to make every effort to move up spiritually through prayer, fasting and personal retreats.

Remedy 4

So it must be clearly understood that seeking and maintaining your personal revival together with all its spiritual and practical benefits both in the present time and in the future must not be conceived as a one day exercise. Rather, it must be seen as a life of continuous prayer, continuous devotional Bible Study and the pursuit and application of constant spiritual principles such as are outlined and discussed above.

Remedy 5

It must finally be seen as a life of constant warfare against backsliding by maintaining vigilance against the infiltrations of all the causes of backsliding which caused even some of the strongest saints to backslide and lose their personal revival as well as their faith in God altogether.

CHAPTER FOUR

UNDERSTANDING AND SEEKING GOD'S PERSONAL REVIVAL REGULARLY (PART 2)

INTRODUCTION

Seeking personal revival is a practical exercise requiring some strenuous efforts guided by some efficient prayer methods. Furthermore, it is a regular prayer exercise requiring some well-defined prayer lines to make it effectual. This very practical aspect of seeking God's regular personal revivals is the major preoccupation of this second chapter on personal revivals. The details can be outlined and discussed as follows:

PRAYING SPECIFIC PERSONAL REVIVAL PRAYERS

Though the main purpose of this section is not to teach the rudiments of prayer again, this teaching on how to pray specific personal revival prayers is still essential in this chapter because its omission will create the wrong impression that we are presuming that everybody who will read this book is mature enough to know how to pray personal revival prayers regularly. This assumption will be wrong because surely, this is a book which will be read by many people with different levels of spiritual maturity. So let us discuss this section with open-mindedness as follows:

I. **We should always start with genuine repentance and confession**

It is always good to begin true personal revival prayers with genuine repentance and heart-felt confession. At a point in time when King David, the great soldier and saint of God realized his sins and shortcomings, he was bold enough to come to his God with penitential prayer.

Psalm 51:1, 4

Have mercy upon me, O God, according to Your lovingkindness; according to the multitude of Your tender mercies, blot out my transgressions. Against You, You only, have I sinned, and done this evil in Your sight — that You may be found just when You speak, and blameless when You judge. NKJV

He was sincere enough to ask God to cleanse him from all his sins. Before the prodigal son could receive the cleansing, forgiveness and restoration, he needed from his father, he also admitted his wrong doing.

Luke 15:21
And the son said to him, 'Father, I have sinned against heaven and in your sight, and am no longer worthy to be called your son.' NKJV

The Bible warns us against pride and self-righteousness when we come into God's presence to seek His cleansing, forgiveness and restoration in Psalm 143:2 with the words:

Psalm 143:2
And enter not into judgment with thy servant: for in thy sight shall no man living be justified. KJV

And do not enter into judgment with Your servant, for in Your sight no man living is righteous or justified. Amplified Bible

There is no one who has ever come before God with genuine repentance and confession who has been rejected. The Bible has no record of any such thing. This truth is emphasized in Psalm 51:17 in the words:

The sacrifice you desire is a broken spirit. You will not reject a broken and repentant heart, O God. NLT

Starting your quest for personal revival with genuine repentance and confession can help you realize your vision in two ways. First, it can help you to deal with any past hidden or overt sins which can be a hindrance to your search for personal revival. Secondly, it will clear your mind and heart of any sin guilt and further grant you the boldness to approach God's throne of grace to ask for His personal revival with great faith. So always start very well with God in your search for personal revival by quoting and standing upon some of the biblical passages on repentance, confession, cleansing and forgiveness such as the following:

Psalm 40:12, 13

For innumerable evils have surrounded me; my iniquities have overtaken me, so that I am not able to look up; they are more than the hairs of my head; therefore my heart fails me. Be pleased, O Lord, to deliver me; O Lord, make haste to help me!

<u>Psalm 51:7</u>
Purge me with hyssop, and I shall be clean; wash me, and I shall be whiter than snow.

To conclude, we want to reemphasize that you can stand on some of the references quoted above on forgiveness, cleansing, renewal and restoration and start your prayer for personal revival on the right note. If you do this very well the ultimate results can be amazing!

II. We should seek personal revival with persistent and continuous prayer

Prayer is the spiritual vehicle which conveys us into God's presence to receive His blessings of power, spiritual renewal and spiritual restoration. So if we truly want to experience God's personal revival regularly and permanently, then the means to this spiritual ideal must be continuous and prevailing prayer. This prayer effort must be the literal fulfilment of 1 Thessalonians 5:17 which reads:

Pray without ceasing. NKJV

Be unceasing and persistent in prayer. Amplified Bible

But what should be the focus of such continuous personal revival prayers? Such prayers must focus on the following important truths outlined below:

1. They must be based upon some of the specific promises of God on His granting personal revival to those who are desirous and serious for it. Some of these promises can be obtained from the following Bible references on revival, renewal and spiritual restoration.

Habakkuk 3:2

O Lord, I have heard Your speech and was afraid; O Lord, revive Your work in the midst of the years! In the midst of the years make it known; in wrath remember mercy. NKJV

Acts 2:17

'And it shall come to pass in the last days, says God, that I will pour out of My Spirit on all flesh; your sons and your daughters shall prophesy, your young men shall see visions, your old men shall dream dreams. NKJV

2 Chronicles 7:14

If My people who are called by My name will humble themselves, and pray and seek My face, and turn from their wicked ways, then I will hear from heaven, and will forgive their sin and heal their land. NKJV

Psalm 85:6

Will You not revive us again, that Your people may rejoice in You? NKJV

Psalm 80:18

Then we will not turn back from You; revive us, and we will call upon Your name. NKJV

Ezekiel 37:3

And He said to me, "Son of man, can these bones live?" So I answered, "O Lord God, You know." NKJV

Psalm 119:25

My soul clings to the dust; revive me according to Your word. NKJV

The prayers for personal revival must be specific and squarely based upon God's word exactly as God has promised in the references quoted above.

If need be, and if so desired, fasting can be added to this prayer for personal revival and renewal. Fasting when added to prayer can strengthen the prayer for personal revival and renewal. It can help us to humble ourselves before God to deny ourselves of our physical needs and help us to focus on seeking this desired spiritual revival and renewal without any side attractions. Futhermore, fasting always helps to create the right spiritual environment for major spiritual transformations to take place. So adding fasting to prayers for general and personal revival is biblical according to Joel 2:12

Joel 2:12
"Now, therefore," says the Lord, "Turn to Me with all your heart, with fasting, with weeping, and with mourning." NKJV

The summary of whatever we have been saying on prayer so far is this: We should continually pray personal revival prayers asking God to bring us His special revival accompanied by His special spiritual renewal which will take us out of perpetual defeat in sin, worldliness and out of all forms of carnality into a renewed high level of spirituality and permanent spiritual renewal.

III. We should Pray continually to be filled with the Holy Spirit

Though God is the divine source of all revivals, He always uses the Holy Spirit as the agent. By analogy, God is the creator of the whole universe. But in creating the world, the Holy Spirit became His chief agent. "In the beginning God created the heavens and the earth. The earth was without form, and void; and darkness was on the face of the deep. And the Spirit of God was hovering over the face of the waters." (Genesis 1:1,2). So God will never grant any personal or group revival anywhere without the active involvement of the Holy Spirit. God being essentially a Spirit being who has never been seen by anybody with the naked eyes always moves and works by His Spirit. Therefore, God's revival minus the Holy Spirit is a practical impossibility.

This is a reminder that we should be conscious to pray for the continuous infilling of the Holy

Spirit anytime we plead with God for His personal or group revival. This explains why one constant significant feature of all revivals and reawakenings in the Bible has always been the mighty outpouring of the Holy Spirit of God to fill His faithful and thoroughly cleansed and sanctified children. In the same way, you cannot avoid the Holy Spirit and get any revival. Consequently, in our prayer for revival and spiritual renewal, we must also make time to pray for the fullness and infilling of the Holy Spirit. This must be done as often as we would pray to God to revive us. Biblical examples of the Spirit's involvement in our revival and renewal can be obtained from the references listed below:

Acts 2:2-4

And suddenly there came a sound from heaven, as of a rushing mighty wind, and it filled the whole house where they were sitting. Then there appeared to them divided tongues, as of fire, and one sat upon each of them. And they were all filled with the Holy Spirit and began to speak with other tongues, as the Spirit gave them utterance. NKJV

<u>Luke 11:13</u>

If you then, being evil, know how to give good gifts to your children, how much more will your heavenly Father give the Holy Spirit to those who ask Him!" NKJV

<u>Ephesians 5:18</u>

And do not be drunk with wine, in which is dissipation; but be filled with the Spirit. NKJV

IV. We should pray for God's personal and practical sanctification

We need holiness and sanctification as preconditions for receiving God's revival. So as we pray for God's personal or group revival as explained in this section, why do we still need to bring in sanctification as one of the major sub-topics? The reason is that continuous personal sanctification is needed both before and after the revival. It is needed before the revival to prepare the ground, mind and heart for the outpouring of God's Spirit to effect the revival. It is also needed after the revival to check backsliding through secret and open sins to help us to maintain the revival. We should always remember that the number one killer of revivals is backsliding. After mighty personal or group revivals, sanctification is needed to help us check and prevent backsliding so that the revival granted by God can be protected to stay with us permanently. So as we pray for personal revival, we must always remember to pray for personal sanctification too.

Let us read the following references to help us:

<u>Leviticus 20:7-8</u>
Consecrate yourselves therefore, and be holy, for I am the Lord your God. And you shall keep My statutes, and perform them: I am the Lord who sanctifies you. NKJV

<u>2 Thessalonians 2:13</u>
But we are bound to give thanks to God always for you, brethren beloved by the Lord, because God from the beginning chose you for salvation through sanctification by the Spirit and belief in the truth. NKJV

<u>1 John 1:5-7</u>

This is the message which we have heard from Him and declare to you, that God is light and in Him is no darkness at all. If we say that we have fellowship with Him, and walk in darkness, we lie and do not practice the truth. But if we walk in the light as He is in the light, we have fellowship with one another, and the blood of Jesus Christ His Son cleanses us from all sin. NKJV

ADOPTING EFFICIENT PROGRAMMES TO SEEK GOD'S PERSONAL REVIVALS REGULARLY

The Bible has a clear pattern for every good and beneficial thing we can do today as Christians. This is why we fully agree with the statement that the Bible is our sure guide in everything. So if something is not in the Bible then it cannot be in the church; neither can it be in the lives of the individual Christians making up the church. After learning all the facts discussed above on praying specific personal revival prayers, every sincere and truly born-again child of God must earnestly desire and seek God's personal revivals regularly as depicted in how some of the saints of God prayed regularly for God's personal revivals in the following references. These references will help us to learn the major facts on the Who, Why, When and How of personal revival prayers. These references can be listed as follows:

EXAMPLES OF PRAYERS FOR PERSONAL REVIVAL

i. Admission of guilt/repentance and confession
    Psalm 139:23, 24
    Search me, O God, and know my heart; try me, and know my anxieties; and see if there is any wicked way in me, and lead me in the way everlasting. NKJV

    Psalm 80:18, 19
    Then we will not turn back from You; revive us, and we will call upon Your name. Restore us, O Lord God of hosts; cause Your face to shine, and we shall be saved! NKJV

ii. Afflictions for lack of personal revival
    Psalm 119:107
    I am afflicted very much; revive me, O Lord, according to Your word. NKJV

    Psalm 119:25

My soul clings to the dust; revive me according to Your word. NKJV

iii. Direct personal revival prayers
<u>Psalm 42:1</u>
As the deer pants for the water brooks, so pants my soul for You, O God. NKJV

<u>Psalms 85:6</u>
Will You not revive us again, that Your people may rejoice in You? NKJV

<u>Habakkuk 3:2</u>
O Lord, I have heard Your speech and was afraid; O Lord, revive Your work in the midst of the years! In the midst of the years make it known; in wrath remember mercy. NKJV

<u>Psalm 119:154</u>
Plead my cause and redeem me; revive me according to Your word. NKJV

iv. Happy results of receiving God's personal revival
<u>Exodus 33:18</u>
And he said, "Please, show me Your glory." NKJV

<u>Psalm 119:50</u>

This is my comfort in my affliction, for Your word has given me life. NKJV

The overall meaning and purpose of this segment is that seeking personal revival must be a normal part of the spiritual life of every faithful disciple and true child of God. The local church becomes spiritually cold, weak and ineffective not only because of the spiritual condition of its leaders but largely because of the spiritual coldness of its general membership who form the majority of this local spiritual workforce as well as the biggest percentage of the local congregation. If every individual church member exerts him/herself spiritually and periodically, there will always be fire in the church! Exercising ourselves individually to be able to remain aglow in the Spirit for the Lord all the time can be done by every faithful church member setting aside one weekend at least every 90 days or less during which he/she alone can fast and pray for deep personal revival leading to spiritual commitment and obedience.

Some churches make this a rule by preparing a schedule based on the day each member was born in a seven-week cycle beginning from Sunday. So in the seven-week period, the first weekend will be for the Sunday borns. The second weekend will be for the Monday borns. This will continue for seven continuous weeks until it comes back to the Sunday borns in the church. While maintaining this general programme in the Church, such churches still encourage their members to add their personal programmes of revival and renewal to this general one.

Churches which use this method of personal but compulsory programme of personal revival and renewal to help their church members individually and the entire church at large stand upon Isaiah 40:29-31 to do this. It reads as follows:

"He gives power to the weak, and to those who have no might He increases strength. Even the youths shall faint and be weary, and the young men shall utterly fall, but those who wait on the Lord shall renew their strength; they shall mount up with wings like eagles, they shall run and not be weary, they shall walk and not faint." NKJV

He gives power to the faint and increases the strength of the weak. Even youths grow tired and weary, and young men stumble and fall. But those who wait upon the LORD will renew their strength; they will mount up with wings like eagles; they will run and not grow weary, they will walk and not faint. Berean Standard Bible

They argue that the Bible is clear on the fact that it is only those who make time to wait upon the Lord through prayer and fasting who get the opportunity to renew their strength regularly. So it is either you wait on the Lord periodically to get this promise of renewal or you become lazy and negligent to lose it and fall into a state of continuous spiritual retrogression.

Before we end this section on adopting efficient programmes to be able to receive and maintain God's personal revival regularly, we want to mention some additional personal prayer activities which can be undertaken to keep you personally revived, strong and powerful all the time. They include the following:

SOME OF THE PRACTICAL RENEWAL PROGRAMMES WE CAN ENGAGE IN TO STAY PERSONALLY REVIVED ALWAYS

1. We can occasionally find some short periods of time to fast and pray specifically for spiritual renewal and spiritual revival. Such as is suggested above during some weekends.

2. When the opportunity presents itself, such as during official public holidays and other incidental holidays, we can find some time either to retreat personally to pray for renewal through prayer and Bible study or retreat with the entire family to engage in this useful spiritual activity.

3. Again, whenever the opportunity presents itself for this to be done such as during long vacations, find some extended periods to engage in revival and renewal prayer activities commonly called long personal retreats. Such retreats can be held alone or together with like-minded believers who are also eager to seek and receive God's personal revival. Jesus has shown us the way by often retreating to be alone with God to pray for renewal, strength and anointing

throughout His earthly ministry. Examples in the gospels are as follows:

<u>Mark 1:35</u>

Now in the morning, having risen a long while before daylight, He went out and departed to a solitary place; and there He prayed. NKJV

<u>Mark 6:46</u>

And when He had sent them away, He departed to the mountain to pray. NKJV

<u>Luke 6:12</u>

Now it came to pass in those days that He went out to the mountain to pray, and continued all night in prayer to God. NKJV

<u>Luke 9:18</u>

And it happened, as He was alone praying, that His disciples joined Him, and He asked them, saying, "Who do the crowds say that I am?" NKJV

<u>Luke 11:1</u>

Now it came to pass, as He was praying in a certain place, when He ceased, that one of His disciples said to Him, "Lord, teach us to pray, as John also taught his disciples." NKJV

4. As a concluding remark, we should remember that it always takes some personal effort and determination to attain all spiritual ideals including the good desire to receive God's personal revivals regularly. There is no cheap road to the treasure house where we can find God's true personal or group revivals. Sometimes, the desires of the flesh must be brought under the control of the Holy Spirit to enable us mount spiritually in personal revival as the following references do emphasize.

<u>Philippians 3:13, 14</u>
Brethren, I do not count myself to have apprehended; but one thing I do, forgetting those things which are behind and reaching forward to those things which are ahead, I press toward the goal for the prize of the upward call of God in Christ Jesus. NKJV

<u>1 Corinthians 9:24-27</u>
Do you not know that those who run in a race all run, but one receives the prize? Run in such a way that you may obtain it. And everyone who competes for the prize is temperate in all things. Now they do it to obtain a perishable crown, but we for an imperishable crown. Therefore I run thus: not with

uncertainty. Thus I fight: not as one who beats the air. But I discipline my body and bring it into subjection, lest, when I have preached to others, I myself should become disqualified. NKJV

<u>Hebrews 12:1, 2</u>
Therefore we also, since we are surrounded by so great a cloud of witnesses, let us lay aside every weight, and the sin which so easily ensnares us, and let us run with endurance the race that is set before us, looking unto Jesus, the author and finisher of our faith, who for the joy that was set before Him endured the cross, despising the shame, and has sat down at the right hand of the throne of God. NKJV

THE IMPORTANCE AND ADVANTAGES OF PERSONAL REVIVAL

1. Personal revival is the basis of all the other levels of revival we can get from God in the local church. Why are we saying this? It is because all important revivals begin with the individuals making up the church before it can spread to others outside the church. It is when the church is filled with people who in their personal walk with God are alive spiritually and are filled with the power and anointing of God that the whole

church can be said to have been revived. **So personal revival is the beginning of every true revival in the church of Christ.**

2. The second major importance of personal revival is that it provides the appropriate channels for God's corporate revival. Before revivals can break out and affect everybody in the church, very often, God first has to send it to some holy and already prepared vessels He can use before it can spread to all others in the church. He got Huldah the prophetess as His holy channel and vessel to use before the revival of her time could start from her to affect everybody in the nation of Israel. (2 Kings 22:14-20)

3. It provides prayer warriors and other human resources for God's revival at the general church level. Revivals are always inseparable from prayer. When some faithful individuals become revived at the personal level, God is able to use them mightily in the prayer for revival until the revival affects everybody in the church. Was it not the powerful prayers of Elijah which brought down God's fire to consume the sacrifice and to bring victory to

God's righteous people as it brought judgement upon the prophets of Baal? Thus, through Elijah's mighty intercessory prayer, the whole of Israel received a mighty visitation from God which brought total defeat to the prophets of Baal as it brought revival and reawakening to the whole of Israel.

4. It is necessary for the spread of revivals into the communities and other churches whenever God's revivals come down. It takes only fire to ignite other fires so when God's revival begins in the local church and it sets its members on fire for Christ, such revived members become God's channels of revival in the community as a whole and are used by the Holy Spirit to spread God's revival wherever they go.

In addition to the above, when the members of a church become fully revived at the personal level, this gives them the impetus to evangelize and share their faith with others in the community. Will this activity not bring great advantages to all the people within the community? Such revived members will catch the attention of all the people in the community who will seek to find out what they have which they lack in their lives and thereby cause them to give their lives to Christ.

5. It propels the work of God and the Great Commission by providing prayerful and Holy Ghost filled workers for the task of evangelism. Every revived individual Christian is potentially a revived soldier of Christ who can penetrate the kingdom of darkness with the word of God to help rescue the lost and perishing.

6. Personal revival leads to the building of spiritually strong family units within the local church. All vibrant churches have such strong family units as the pillars and columns of the church. As long as these families persist in the church and pass on the teachings and traditions of the Christ to the younger members of the family, the local church remains strong all the time to be able to work to help fulfil the Great Commission and further impact their communities for Christ.

QUOTED PASSAGES ON "PERSONAL REVIVAL" FROM SOME AUTHENTIC CHRISTIAN SOURCES

BROKENNESS THE PATH TO PERSONAL REVIVAL

Verse 14 says, "If my people, which are called by my name, shall humble themselves, and pray, and seek my face, and turn from their wicked ways; then will I hear from heaven, and will forgive their sin, and will heal their land."

...I discovered that while God may not give a wide spread revival to His people in a given locality of the earth, He will give personal revival to the individual anywhere anytime. But what God chooses to withhold from the country, He will not withhold from the individual who is willing to seek Him.

Our text, though an Old Testament text that applies to the nation of Israel, is a good text to show the way to personal revival. It is the way of brokenness. This is a term that has been adopted by those who have been used of God to teach the way to personal revival.

The American Heritage Dictionary defines brokenness: "Subdued totally." It is an attitude of humility that comes from the recognition of our powerlessness to meet God's standards in ourselves. It is a submission to God's viewpoint; it is a transparency about sin when it arises and bowing before God at the cross. A man is broken when he is willing to walk in the light and confess his sins as they arise (1 John 1:6-9).

I personally believe that every saved person has experienced personal revival. It happened when we were first saved. It may have not lasted long but we can remember the overflowing joy that we experienced. During that time we were back under the authority of the Throne. What He said made a big difference to us. Revival comes from God. It is not something worked up, it is prayed down.

We do not have to wait on widespread revival. We can have revival daily on a personal basis. The conditions are clearly laid out through the Scriptures. What we need is personal revival while we wait and pray for a nationwide revival.

By Dr. Earl White

PERSONAL REVIVAL

Like a mighty wave rolling across the church around the world, comes the cry from millions of believers, "O God, send a revival!" Like no time in recent history, the church is becoming aware of its own desperate condition and the even more critical needs of our cultures.

What is it we are praying for when we ask God to send revival? Some of my favorite short definitions of revival are:

"…a movement of the Holy Spirit bringing about a revival of New Testament Christianity in the church of Christ and its related community." – J. Edwin Orr

"Revival is a community saturated with God." – Duncan Campbell

"Revival is the church falling in love with Jesus all over again." – Vance Havner

Perhaps the one that best fits my own understanding is from Stephen Olford, who says, "Revival is ultimately Christ Himself, seen, felt, heard, living, active, moving in and through His Body on earth."

Much has been written on what happens when revival touches a church, community or nation. Foundational to each of those spheres of revival is a fresh touch from Christ upon an individual. J. Edwin Orr speaks of those different spheres this way: "Such an awakening may

change in a significant way an individual; or it may affect a larger group of believers; or it may move a congregation or the churches in the city or district, or the body of believers throughout a country or continent; or indeed, the larger body of believers throughout the world."

Paul would go so far as to say, "...I no longer live, but Christ lives in me..." (Gal. 2:20). True spiritual awakening begins on a personal basis as we begin to live out daily the truth of God's Word,

By Dave Butts

DO YOU WANT PERSONAL REVIVAL TOO?

What is revival?

In his sermon on Sunday, February 20, pastor Jack Hibbs clarified that revival means that something that is alive— is made alive again.

New Life vs. Personal Revival
Personal revival occurs when we allow the Holy Spirit's conviction to transform us from a life that looks less than alive to one that is vibrant and has impact for God's Kingdom. We get rid of all the dirt and grime from the

flashlight. Now, when we turn it on, it shines a briht beam, illuminating the darkness.

How We Can Experience Personal Revival I think personal revival begins with recognizing and understanding the gravity of what Christ did for us. The penalty for our sin is death–eternal separation from God in everlasting torment. But God does not want us to experience His wrath over sin; He loves us. He sent His one and only Son, Jesus, to pay the penalty for our sin. He died. Then He rose to life again! Thus purchasing salvation for us. In addition, experiencing revival begins with asking the Holy Spirit to reveal unconfessed sin in our lives.

Revival will be reflected when we …

1. *Turn away from thinking patterns, habits, and activities that are not God-honoring. Pursue holiness. Not the kind that makes people uncomfortable. But a life that shines love and kindness (Philippians 2:14-15).*

2. *Seek forgiveness from anyone we have sinned against. And forgive those who have wounded us (Ephesians 4:32). In addition, we can pray that God will give us more sensitivity so that we are not easily offended. (Proverbs 19:11).*

3. *Move into bolder Christian living. Look for opportunities to share the gospel with people in your circle of influence (Romans 10:14-15).*
By Dianne Thornton

STEPHEN ADU-BOAHEN